WORTHY OF THE KINGDOM

(Insights for Daily Living from Second Thessalonians)

THOMAS R. HENDERSHOT

Unless otherwise indicated, all Scripture is from the World English Bible (WEB). The World English Bible (WEB) is a Public Domain (no copyright) Modern English translation of the Holy Bible. The WEB is annotated throughout this book when I have listed a passage with more than one translation together.

Other Versions used are:

Scripture quotations noted AMP are taken from the Amplified® Bible, Copyright © 1954, 1958, 1962, 1964, 1965, 1987 by The Lockman Foundation. Used by permission. (www.Lockman.org).

Scripture quotations marked (ESV) are from the Holy Bible, English Standard Version ® (ESV), copyright 2001 by Crossway Bibles, a publishing ministry of Good News Publishers. Used by permission. All rights reserved.

Scripture quotations marked (KJV) are from the King James Version.

Scripture marked (MEV) is taken from the Modern English Version, Copyright © 2014 by Military Bible Association. Used by permission. All rights reserved.

Scripture quotations marked (NASB) are taken from the NEW AMERICAN STANDARD BIBLE®, Copyright © 1960, 1962, 1963, 1968, 1971, 1972, 1973, 1975, 1977, 1995 by The Lockman Foundation. Used by permission."

Scripture quotations marked (NKJV) are taken from the New King James Version® (NKJV), Copyright © 1982 by Thomas Nelson, Inc. Used by permission. All rights reserved.

Copyright © 2015 Thomas R. Hendershot
All rights reserved.
ISBN-10:   1512350567
ISBN-13:   978-1512350562

DEDICATION

To my dad, Walt.

CONTENTS

	PREFACE	vii
1	KINGDOM AFFIRMATION	Pg # 1
2	KINGDOM AWARENESS	Pg # 21
3	KINGDOM ADVICE	Pg # 47

PREFACE

The Apostle Paul wrote a letter to the believers in Thessalonica. Later he wrote a second letter to clarify some things they had misunderstood about his previous letter and teaching, and to correct some erroneous ideas that false teachers had spread in his name.

The second letter is shorter than the first but is no less powerful. I have divided the three short chapters into three subjects: *Affirmation* concerning their faith and sufferings, *Awareness* of the coming Man of Lawlessness, and *Advice* concerning proper Christian living. The affirmation, awareness, and advice given here is no less applicable to us now than it was to them. "May God so grant that we read, pray, be changed into the image of Christ and become ones who are worthy of the Kingdom of God. Amen."

THOMAS R. HENDERSHOT

1

KINGDOM AFFIRMATION

DAY ONE: "Activation."

Today let's activate our faith by taking a brief look at chapter one of Second Thessalonians. In this chapter, Paul affirmed the faith of these believers, giving thanks for them. Paul encouraged them in their hardships. He declared them worthy of the Kingdom. He confirmed the truth to them that God is righteous and will give relief to them in their affliction and deal with those who trouble them. He activated their faith in the King and the Kingdom of Righteousness. We can certainly learn a lot from reading this chapter and should carefully apply its truth to our lives. Let's make this our goal as we go forward.

CLOSING WORD: "¹**Paul and Silvanus and Timothy, to the church of the Thessalonians in God our Father and the Lord Jesus Christ: ²Grace to you and peace from God the Father and the Lord Jesus Christ. ³We ought always to give thanks to God for you, brethren, as is *only* fitting, because your faith is greatly enlarged, and the love of each one of you** toward one another grows *ever* greater; ⁴ therefore, we ourselves speak proudly of you among the churches of God for your perseverance and faith in the midst of all your persecutions and afflictions which you endure. ⁵ *This is* a plain indication of God's righteous judgment so that you will be considered worthy of the kingdom of God, for which indeed you are suffering. ⁶ For after all it is *only* just for God to repay with affliction those who afflict you, ⁷ and *to give* relief to you who are afflicted and to us as well when the Lord Jesus will be revealed from heaven with His mighty angels in flaming fire, ⁸ dealing out retribution to those who do not know God and to those who do not obey the gospel of our Lord Jesus. ⁹ These will pay the penalty of eternal destruction, away from the presence of the Lord and from the glory of His power, ¹⁰ when He comes to be glorified in His saints on that day, and to be marveled at among all who have believed—for our testimony to you was believed. ¹¹ To this end also we pray for you always, that our God will count you worthy of your calling, and fulfill every desire for goodness and the work of faith with power, ¹² so that the name of our Lord Jesus will be glorified in you, and you in Him, according to the grace of our God and *the* Lord Jesus Christ." (2 Thessalonians 1:1-12)

PRAYER: "Father, as I begin this exciting study in Your Word, help me to hear what Your Holy Spirit is speaking to me. Help me to receive the truth of the Kingdom and grow in faith during my trials. Open my mind and understanding to comprehend Your instruction to me. Open my heart to commit my life afresh to You in complete and unreserved obedience. I ask this through Jesus Christ, the King of kings and Lord of lords. Amen."

DAY TWO: "Apostolic Authority."

""Paul and Silvanus and Timothy, to the church of the Thessalonians in God our Father and the Lord Jesus Christ." (1:1).

All three of these men were apostles. Paul wrote this letter with the force of his apostolic authority. *Affirmation* was one of the features of the ministry and gifting of the Apostles. Jesus said we would come into the right knowledge of Him through the words of His chosen apostles (John 17:20). We are affirmed and blessed when we listen to and obey the words of those whom God has called to teach us.

In my book, "Worshiping, Working, and Waiting," I noted that First Thessalonians was likely the first letter that Paul wrote to a church of which we have a record of. According to scholars, Second Thessalonians is the second Paul wrote. There are similarities and some clarification of the earlier correspondence as it is the sequel.

The first letter was written more for encouragement. However, Paul is more corrective here as he addressed some inaccurate and false information that was circulating among them and some practical issues about the way they lived. Second Thessalonians provides us with an excellent look at some of the questions and issues that concerned the early Christians. Many of these subjects are concerns of us today too.

Notice also, even though Paul was an apostle with much authority, he did not work in a vacuum. Closely connected to him were both Silas and Timothy. This is a crucial point. Regardless of the greatness of one's gifting, we lose ground for the Kingdom when we do not connect with other leaders. The synergy of these apostles produced greater results than any of them could have alone. Let us deliberately connect with the Apostles through their words here and with others of faith around us in our time.

CLOSING WORD: "[20]I do not ask on behalf of these alone, but for those also who believe in Me through their word; [21] that they may all be one; even as You, Father, *are* in Me and I in You, that they also may be in Us, so that the world may believe that You sent Me. [22]The glory which You have given Me I have given to them, that they may be one, just as We are one; [23]I in them and You in Me, that they may be perfected in unity, so that the world may know that You sent Me, and loved them, even as You have loved Me." (John 17:20-23)

PRAYER: "Father, I thank You that You gave the truth to Your Apostles, and they recorded it. We are built on the foundation of the Apostles and Prophets, Jesus Christ, Your Son being the Chief Corner Stone. I thank You that we have what they wrote today, and can read it. Show me how to connect with this truth and to others around me to advance Your Kingdom in my world. I ask this in Your holy name, Amen."

DAY THREE: "And."

"In God our Father and the Lord Jesus Christ..." (1:2)

In a display of perfect unity, Paul greeted them saying it was from Himself **and** Silas, **and** Timothy in God our Father **and** the Lord Jesus Christ. The unity of these three apostles is in the oneness of God and Jesus. That is a powerful unity. It is a oneness of purpose, message, and spirit.

Here Paul called God, "our Father." He is not only the Father of Jesus. He is the Father of every believer. We have been included in the family too. It is the one family of God (Ephesians 2:18-22, 3:15).

Paul called God their Father because of the salvation they had received through Jesus Christ. God was their Father because of His Son. The work of Christ on the cross made salvation available for those who believed.

He is our Father too if we come to Him through the merits of His unique Son, Jesus. He goes on to show that grace and peace were given to them because of the Father and the Son. The Father and the Son have always existed in perfect unity and oneness and have acted in time by grace, bringing peace. Let us receive the blessings of the Father and the Son.

CLOSING WORD: "*⁴There is* one body and one Spirit, just as also you were called in one hope of your calling; ⁵ one Lord, one faith, one baptism, ⁶ one God and Father of all who is over all and through all and in all." (Ephesians 4:4-6)

PRAYER: "Holy Father, You have acted on my behalf because of the work of Your Son, Jesus, my Lord. Teach me to follow You in the unity of the Spirit with my fellow believers. Amen."

DAY FOUR: "Always."

"**We ought always to give thanks to God for you, brethren, as is *only* fitting, because your faith is greatly enlarged, and the love of each one of you toward one another grows *ever* greater.**" (1:3)

Gratitude is one sure way to know whether or not someone has truly received the grace of God. When we receive the grace of God, we should become full of thankfulness. When we truly see it manifested in others, we cannot help but to rejoice in it. We are compelled to give thanks. We feel obligated to thank God for what He has done. That is the normal spiritual response toward God if we have even a basic level of understanding of what has happened in our life and the life of other's.

But this is often not the case. Many times folks receive blessings and are not thankful. The truth is; the ones who are not thankful don't last. The grateful believers are the ones that last. Thankfulness is a fruit of a grateful heart.

It is not a hit and miss situation here. It is a continual flow of the Spirit. In the first letter to these believers, Paul told them to be thankful for everything (5:18). This attitude is always God's will for us. It is fitting to thank God for the growing faith of others. We are bound to be thankful always. If we are continually grateful for folks, we will appreciate them more and grow closer to them.

CLOSING WORD: "**⁶ As therefore you received Christ Jesus, the Lord, walk in him, ⁷ rooted and built up in him, and established in the faith,** even as you were taught, abounding in it in thanksgiving." (Colossians 2:6-7)

PRAYER: "Father, I give thanks today for every blessing You have given me and for all of the brothers and sisters in Christ You have put into my life. Amen."

DAY FIVE: "As is Only Fitting."

"We ought always to give thanks to God for you, brethren, as is *only* fitting, because your faith is greatly enlarged, and the love of each one of you toward one another grows *ever* greater." (1:3)

Our faith can grow. That's good news. If my faith is not as strong as I want it to be, I can be encouraged because of this verse. These believers grew a lot in their faith. Their faith was greatly enlarged. There is a great potential in this passage.

How does our faith grow? One way is through understanding. God's truth is the foundation of real faith. As believers receive the truth, they must continually seek an understanding of it. We should pray for more understanding (Proverbs 4:7, John 8:31-32).

Another way faith grows is through action. Real faith moves a person to do what God has instructed. Obedience is the test of faith. God gives us instructions to follow. As we obey His instructions, our faith increases (2 Kings 5:14, James 2:22, 1 Peter 1:13).

CLOSING WORD: "**'The apostles said to the Lord, "Increase our faith."'** (Luke 17:5)

PRAYER: "O Lord, increase my faith. Give me understanding and the will to obey You in all things. In the Name of Jesus Christ, the Lord, I ask this. Amen."

DAY SIX: "Always and One Another."

"We ought always to give thanks to God for you, brethren, as is *only* fitting, because your faith is greatly enlarged, and the love of each one of you toward one another grows *ever* greater." (1:3)

Paul called them brethren. This is a familial term. Believers are family. Families care for one another. Love is meant to be shared. The Apostles shared the love of Christ with these folks. They shared it with each other and subsequently grew in love. Therefore, they became greater and greater in faith and love. When folks make this their manner of life, they are living the abundant life Jesus promised to His followers.

This is why the Apostle John told believers to walk in the love of God toward one another (1 John 4:7-8). It proves our faith. Our faith grows as we operate by the love of God (Galatians 5:6). Sometimes we have to love by faith. If we do, God helps us to grow in both love and faith. We must be diligent to maintain ourselves in the love of God (Jude 1:21). When we live this way, we fulfill all of the demands of the law of the Old Testament (Romans 13:10). This doesn't mean we keep all of the details of the Old Testament law. It means we fulfill the intention of it by walking in love.

CLOSING WORD: **"This is my commandment, that you love one another, even as I have loved you."** (John 15:12)

PRAYER: "Dear Lord Jesus, teach me to walk in love according to Your Word and will in my life. Show me where I have failed and motivate me to go forward walking in Your love toward all. In Your name, I pray. Amen."

DAY SEVEN: "All Your Persecutions and Afflictions."

"Therefore, we ourselves speak proudly of you among the churches of God for your perseverance and faith in the midst of all your persecutions and afflictions which you endure." (1:4)

It can be difficult to love others when they are abusing us. It requires a serious commitment to God and love for others. It is not natural to us to endure hardship. We want to retaliate and get justice in the here and now. It takes great faith to trust God and to love our enemies.

Every believer needs to develop perseverance. In our modern culture, we don't seem to have much endurance along these lines. But faith and patience work hand in hand (Hebrews 6:11-12). Trials, tribulations, and afflictions will develop us in the areas of perseverance, proven character, and hope (Romans 5:3-5). The Holy Spirit will lead us into challenges to develop our faith and prove us (Matthew 4:1, 1 Peter 1:7).

God wants to develop us in our endurance. Often our suffering is not a strange thing; It is a God thing (1 Peter 4:12). Jesus left an example of suffering for us, and He calls us to follow in His steps (1 Peter 2:21). We must consider how God is developing us in this way. We should ask Him for wisdom during our trials. We can trust Him that the end will be better than when we started (Job 23:10, Romans 8:28, James 5:10-11).

CLOSING WORD: "**²Count it all joy, my brothers, when you fall into various temptations, ³ knowing that the testing of your faith produces endurance. ⁴Let endurance have its perfect work, that you may be perfect and complete, lacking in nothing. ⁵But if any of you lacks wisdom, let him ask of God, who gives to all liberally and without reproach; and it will be given to him.**" (James 1:2-5)

PRAYER: "Dear Father, I repent for often complaining about my situations. Strengthen me to endure hardship as a good soldier of Jesus Christ and to let the spiritual fruit of patience do its work in me developing me into the mature believer You have called me to be in Christ. Amen."

DAY EIGHT: "A Plain Indication."

"*This is* a plain indication of God's righteous judgment so that you will be considered worthy of the kingdom of God, for which indeed

you are suffering." (1:5)

Jesus is King now. He has won the victory. He rules and reigns now spiritually and is King of all the earth. His kingdom is still advancing across the earth in our time. God wants to establish His Kingdom in our time and our world further. It goes forward in many ways. Sometimes we miss it because we narrow its advancement by only looking at it in a narrow sense.

In this passage, we learn that one of the ways His Kingdom advances is as we suffer properly for righteousness sake. That's not suffering because of our sinful actions (1 Peter 4:14-19). It is suffering because of the name of Christ. The Spirit of God rests upon us in a special way when we suffer in this manner. There is a special empowering of God for us connected with this.

Paul was giving them an affirming word in their suffering. The Spirit comes to cause Jesus to be glorified through our afflictions. Then it is a powerful witness of the Kingdom of God. "O God, make us worthy of such a powerful witness" (Acts 1:8).

The plain indication of God's judgment on the Last Day is manifested in time when the righteous endure persecution on earth. We must enter the Kingdom of God through the doorway of tribulation (Acts 14:22). Paul was confirming their faith when telling them this.

The race of faith is not about who begins, but who finishes (Hebrews 12:1-4). It was plain to Paul that these believers were of the Kingdom of God. They were considered worthy of the Kingdom because they suffered through affliction while keeping their faith (Revelation 12:11). They suffered for Christ. God declared them worthy because of the sufferings of Jesus. They suffered for Christ because God declared them worthy in Christ. They had His nature. They were partakers of His sufferings. They were one with Him. Therefore, they were sold out for the Kingdom.

The ones who are sold out for Christ are obvious. They are a powerful testimony in the earth to the righteous judgment of God. The Greek word for witness is *martyr* (Acts 1:8). God counted them worthy to suffer as He saw fit to advance the Kingdom. Let us season our generation by suffering successfully while promoting the Kingdom of God in our time.

CLOSING WORD: **"[11]Blessed are you when people reproach you, persecute you, and say all kinds of evil against you falsely, for my sake. [12]Rejoice, and be exceedingly glad, for great is your reward in heaven. For that is how they persecuted the prophets who were before you. [13]"You are the salt of the earth, but if the salt has lost its flavor, with what will it be salted? It is then good for nothing, but to be cast out and trodden under the feet of men."** (Matthew 5:11-13)

PRAYER: "Dear Father, strengthen me by the power of Jesus Christ and do Your work in me that others can see plainly that I am worthy of Your Kingdom by the sufferings of Jesus Christ being manifested in my life. Use my life to advance Your Kingdom. Thy kingdom come. Thy will be done. Amen."

DAY NINE: "After All."

"[6]For after all it is *only* just for God to repay with affliction those who afflict you, [7] and *to give* relief to you who are afflicted and to us as well when the Lord Jesus will be revealed from heaven with His mighty angels in flaming fire, [8] dealing out retribution to those who do not know God and to those who do not obey the gospel of our Lord Jesus." (1:6-8)

The believer must not seek revenge. God is just. He has and will establish His justice in every time of history. We are not called to hate our enemies. We are called to love them. Vengeance is the Lord's business, not ours. Jesus set the example on the cross, praying for the forgiveness of those who had been so brutal to Him. A reckoning always comes. After all, the Judge of the whole earth will do what is right (Genesis 18:25). He stands at the door and executes His judgment at the proper time (James 5:9). We must be patient and give glory to God even in our hardships. He gives His children relief in His time (Hebrews 10:30-31). Also, don't forget, there will be a reckoning in the end.

This does not mean the believer should sit back and do nothing. We are to "occupy until He comes" (Luke 19:13). We should do our best to be salt in the earth and the light of the world in our time (Matthew 5:13-16). We should seek to advance the Kingdom of God in any and every way possible.

However, we know what else often comes with this territory. Some folks are evil and will oppose God's plan and people. These are the ones who often persecute the saints for doing God's will on the earth. We must continue to do the right thing even when they persecute us for doing it. We leave the vengeance part with God.

CLOSING WORD: "**[17]Repay no one evil for evil. Respect what is honorable in the sight of all men. [18]If it is possible, as much as it is up to you, be at peace with all men. [19]Don't seek revenge yourselves, beloved, but give place to God's wrath. For it is written, "Vengeance belongs to me; I will repay, says the Lord." [20] Therefore "If your enemy is hungry, feed him. If he is thirsty, give him a drink; for in doing so, you will heap coals of fire on his head." [21]Don't be overcome by evil, but overcome evil with good.**" (Romans 12:17-21)

PRAYER: "Lord, teach me to do the right thing with the right motives. Empower me to help advance the Kingdom in the areas You have called me to. Help me to not retaliate inappropriately when I am challenged by evil forces. Give me wisdom to fight spiritual battles with spiritual weapons and earthly opposition with understanding, courage, and compassion. I ask this in Your name, O Sovereign Lord and King. Amen."

DAY TEN: "As Well."

"And *to give* relief to you who are afflicted and to us as well." (1:7a)

Spiritual law teaches us that "humans reap what they have planted." This law applies whether for good or bad (Galatians 6:7-9). Those who afflict others get what is coming to them. This is a principle that takes care of itself. We do not need ever to pursue it. The one who sows the wind will reap the whirlwind (Hosea 8:7).

Some are appointed to office to execute the laws. This is natural human government and is necessary for the order. We can't become the law, judge and jury on our own. For our part, generally we are best to leave that to the ones appointed. The spiritual law informs us.

As well, all men are required to obey God. Not just the church folks. The Kingdom of God covers the entire earth. God will bless and punish the whole world according to how they follow His commandments. All men will stand before Jesus to give an account for the deeds done in the body, whether good or bad (2 Corinthians 5:10). "All men" means saints and sinners. What we do matters, and we will give an account for it. The outcome of that final judgment will certainly be different for the believer and the unrepentant sinner. But the fact remains, the Judgment Day awaits all. He has given us His law and way and requires all men to submit to it.

God's commandments are not meant to be a grievous burden for us. They are meant to be a blessing. In whatever ways even the wicked obey His laws, they are blessed in those areas. God is not mocked. He blesses humanity according to their obedience to His precepts. If we want a better home, school, community, or world, we must promote and establish His ways. All men will stand and fall based off of the laws of God.

God's laws are not mere suggestions. Sometimes even believers consider the commandments of God as suggestions. That's foolishness. The Ten Commandments are the ten words of life. Every part of God's dealings with humanity has been to help us. The whole thing applies to the whole world. The entire Bible is the inspired Word of God and is useful for all of life.

THE WORD FOR TODAY: "**¹⁶All Scripture is inspired by God and is profitable for teaching, for reproof, for correction, and for instruction in righteousness, ¹⁷ that the man of God may be complete, thoroughly equipped for every good work.**" (2 Timothy 3:16:17, MEV)

PRAYER: "Heavenly Father, I thank You for Your Word. Teach me to follow it faithfully and to be a definite change agent in my world. I ask this in Jesus' name. Amen."

DAY ELEVEN: "Angels."

"**When the Lord Jesus will be revealed from heaven with His mighty angels in flaming fire, dealing out retribution to those who do not know God and to those who do not obey the gospel of our Lord Jesus.**" (1:7b-8)

Angels are actively involved in the universe. At times, they are God's messengers. They are warriors in the spiritual realm for the Kingdom of God. They will have an active role at the end of time. Saints and angels will play a part in Christ's work of judgment (Matthew 19:28, 25:31, 1 Corinthians 6:2-3). The final judgment of God will set things right. Evil men will receive from God the due recompense of their dealings with God's people. I believe the Angels will have a role in this.

We have a mighty force with us on the side of righteousness. Angels are with God's people. They protect the saints. We are never alone. The forces of evil are not greater than the forces of good. Sometimes they intervene in human affairs. They will indeed be involved with God's execution of His final vengeance in the end. Jesus will be revealed from heaven and will repay all evil. The

Angels will accompany Him. This aspect of the judgment is yet future. Christians believe in a Judgment Day after the Second Coming of Christ and the Resurrection. Let us be ready for it.

THE WORD FOR TODAY: **"But when the Son of Man comes in his glory, and all the holy angels with him, then he will sit on the throne of his glory."** (Matthew 25:31)

PRAYER: "Father, I glorify You and thank You for the ministry of Your holy angels. I believe You help me now and Your angels minister to the saints. I understand that You will set things right on the final Judgment Day. For now, I trust Your wisdom. In the last hour, I rest in Your mercy. Help me to worship You in Your majesty. Amen."

DAY TWELVE: "Appearance from Heaven."

"When the Lord Jesus will be revealed from heaven with His mighty angels in flaming fire, dealing out retribution to those who do not know God and to those who do not obey the gospel of our Lord Jesus." (1:7b-8)

A day of final judgment will come. No one knows when. But God also judges in time. History reveals instances and places. He judged Israel in AD 70. He came to them in judgment. He has judged other nations throughout history. He has executed judgment on individuals throughout history. He is righteous and sovereign. Jesus is the King, who has come. He is the King now. He is the coming King. He is Lord of all. The earth is His. He rules everything.

Jesus will return at the end and a great Day of Judgment will occur. The mighty Lord of glory will execute judgment on those who have refused to know God and have rejected His offer of grace. The Son of God will be revealed from heaven in glory. They who have afflicted God's people will be punished. God is righteous. He will not ignore the sufferings of His elect. The main idea here is that this is an eternal judgment that will happen one day. The demands of the gospel of grace must be heeded. All who reject this will be eternally punished. All who oppose God's people will be judged for their actions. A just God must punish evil in order to reward good. Our God is just and right.

CLOSING WORD: "**[16] But if one of you suffers for being a Christian, let him not be ashamed; but let him glorify God in this matter. [17] For the time has come for judgment to begin with the household of God. If it begins first with us, what will happen to those who don't obey the Good News of God? [18] "If it is hard for the righteous to be saved, what will happen to the ungodly and the sinner?" [19] Therefore let them also who suffer according to the will of God in doing good entrust their souls to him, as to a faithful Creator.**" (1 Peter 4:16-19)

PRAYER: "Father, I know the Day of Judgment is coming. Make me ready. Help me to do my part in rescuing others from destruction. Help me to leave judgment in these matters to You. Come, Lord Jesus. Come! Amen"

DAY THIRTEEN: "Away from the Presence."

"**[9]These will pay the penalty of eternal destruction, away from the presence of the Lord and from the glory of His power, [10] when He comes to be glorified in His saints on that day, and to be marveled at among all who have believed—for our testimony to you was believed.**" (1:9-10)

Possibly the worse punishment in eternity is the absolute removal of one from God's presence. The punishment of evil doers is eternal. It is destruction. It is the departure of His glory. It is the blackness of darkness forever.

Today is the Day of Salvation. Believers must call unbelievers to repentance. Saints must live in constant watchfulness for the Lord's return from heaven (Acts 1:11, Matthew 24:42). The return of Jesus is the promise of a God who never breaks His word. It is the next great event of which every believer should live in expectation. Jesus is coming again. Even so, come, Lord Jesus!

CLOSING WORD: "**Watch therefore, for you don't know in what hour your Lord comes.**" (Matt. 24:42)

PRAYER: "Our Father, Your Word to the disciples of Jesus was to "watch and pray." Help me to be sober and watch for all that is yet to come upon the earth, both glorious and judgmental. Make me wise enough to see the balance of Your sovereign care. We know that good will ultimately receive reward and evil receive its punishment. You are just. Help me to live with the expectation that the King, who is coming, will do what is right. Give me opportunities and wisdom to call sinners to repentance. In Jesus' name! Amen"

DAY FOURTEEN: "Also and Always."

"[11]To this end also we pray for you always, that our God will count you worthy of your calling, and fulfill every desire for goodness and the work of faith with power, [12] so that the name of our Lord Jesus will be glorified in you, and you in Him, according to the grace of our God and *the* Lord Jesus Christ." (1:11-12)

The previous verses yesterday confirm to us that evil will receive its judgment. Those who persecute God's people will receive retribution from God's own hand. The call of God for these believers was to be thankful for God's blessings, His presence in their present struggle, and to be confident of His glorious purpose for them. Paul spoke these words when with them, wrote to them to encourage them, and prayed for them always to this end.

There are similar distresses and challenges in most of our lives. However, every believer is called to walk a path that will have its own unique challenges due to the time, location, and so on. The challenges for the Thessalonians were somewhat unique. But the ultimate goal in every believer's life is to bring glory to God. "May we all be worthy of this."

CLOSING WORD: "**⁹ For this cause, we also, since the day we heard this, don't cease praying and making requests for you, that you may be filled with the knowledge of his will in all spiritual wisdom and understanding, ¹⁰ that you may walk worthily of the Lord, to please him in all respects, bearing fruit in every good work, and increasing in the knowledge of God;..**" (Colossians 1:9-10)

PRAYER: "Dear Lord Jesus, help me to live for You as I should in this place and during this time. I also pray for my fellow believers. Fill us with the knowledge of Your will and all spiritual wisdom and understanding, that we may all walk worthy of the Lord, pleasing You and bearing fruit. Amen."

DAY FIFTEEN: "According to Grace."

"**¹¹To this end also we pray for you always, that our God will count you worthy of your calling, and fulfill every desire for goodness and the work of faith with power, ¹² so that the name of our Lord Jesus will be glorified in you, and you in Him, according to the grace of our God and *the* Lord Jesus Christ.**" (1:11-12)

It may sound overwhelming for us to talk about being worthy of the Kingdom and walking worthy of the Lord. That's reasonable since it is impossible to do this in our own power. But according to the grace of God we can do it. We are people of grace and, therefore, worthy of the Kingdom and our calling, through Christ.

I did not comment specifically on the word "worthy" earlier on Day Eight, as the devotion for that day was already lengthy. Here in verse 11, the word "worthy" is again used. Let's take a few minutes and look at this word.

In verse 5 it is "*considered* worthy" (the meaning is the courtroom sense of a judicial verdict.) This is used in verse 5 primarily in the sense of God's declaration on the Day of Judgment that His people are not guilty and because they are connected with Jesus not to be punished. They prove this by their work and tribulation in the Kingdom. They suffer faithfully because Christ has made them worthy. Their sufferings prove that they have been made worthy.

Here in verse 11 it is "*count* worthy." This verse elaborates further on the meaning of verse 5. So the meaning is this: "You are counted worthy of your calling and the Kingdom through grace because of Jesus, the King." "You will be counted worthy of the Kingdom of God when Jesus returns in power and glory because you lived by this grace."

Therefore, the believers in Thessalonica must live worthy of the call of God and His Kingdom. This means living in the Kingdom in the here and now with a Kingdom expectation for eternity. This kind of living brings glory to God.

CLOSING WORD: "**[14] You are the light of the world. A city located on a hill can't be hidden. [15] Neither do you light a lamp, and put it under a measuring basket, but on a stand; and it shines to all who are in the house. [16] Even so, let your light shine before men; that they may see your good works, and glorify your Father who is in heaven**" (Matthew 5:14-16).

PRAYER: "Father, I thank You for saving me through grace on the merits of Jesus. I know You didn't save me only for the purpose of taking me to heaven. I acknowledge You have a purpose for me here and now. Grant me to walk by Your grace and be considered and counted worthy of my calling and of Your Kingdom. Let my light shine in the darkness of the world around me that I might bring glory to You. Amen."

DAY SIXTEEN: "Affirmation and Action."

The power of God's Word is activated as we read, study, and meditate on it, and the Holy Spirit makes it a reality in our life by the grace of God. Let us affirm the truth and seek for ways in which God can activate it within our lives.

THE WORD FOR TODAY: **"⁸For by grace you have been saved through faith, and that not of yourselves; it is the gift of God, ⁹ not of works, that no one would boast. ¹⁰For we are his workmanship, created in Christ Jesus for good works, which God prepared before that we would walk in them."** (Ephesians 2:8-10)

PRAYER: "Gracious Father, I come to You today not on my own merit, but on the perfect life and holiness of Jesus, my Savior. Show me today ways I can increase in understanding and operate in the calling You have for me in my life. Reveal the purpose of Your Kingdom in my time. Activate me toward Your Kingdom goals. In Christ's name, I ask this. Amen."

THE WORD IN ACTION:

Identify the Kingdom truth God Has affirmed in you during this study of His Word:

_____
_____
_____
_____
_____
_____
_____
_____
_____
_____
_____
_____
_____
_____

Dear Father, please show me how You want to activate this truth in my daily life:

2

KINGDOM AWARENESS

DAY SEVENTEEN: "Activation."

Today let's get more familiar with chapter two of Second Thessalonians. In this chapter, Paul revealed more specifics regarding the Second Coming of Christ. He dealt specifically with the false narrative that the Day of the Lord had already come by showing that some of the events on God's timetable hadn't occurred yet. The primary emphasis to that point concerned the Man of Lawlessness.

The subject of the Man of Lawlessness is a difficult one. I will share my opinion after thirty-five plus years of studying this passage. I do not adhere to the fundamentalist, dispensational interpretation. I do not adhere to the hyper-preterist stance. My view is what I believe to be a moderate view that neither ignores the futuristic implications nor swims in the waters of the overreach found in ultra-literalists. I do not claim perfect knowledge of every aspect of this passage. While I would side closer to the Preterist position, their claim that this refers to Nero alone and has already been fulfilled doesn't adequately solve the puzzle of the text. Also, some saying the Antichrist is only the spiritual opposition the Christian faces ignores certain parts of what Paul said that are difficult to explain by spiritualizing too much.

There are certainly spiritual aspects relating to this text. But there are also literal parts that can't be denied and shouldn't be ignored. There is also an impending component to the passage that places it during the time of the Second Coming of Jesus. Consequently, for me, this future aspect embedded in the context of this chapter has not yet been fulfilled. See if you agree with me on this as you read this passage and ask the Holy Spirit to guide your understanding.

CLOSING WORD: "¹Now we request you, brethren, with regard to the coming of our Lord Jesus Christ and our gathering together to Him, ²that you not be quickly shaken from your composure or be disturbed either by a spirit or a message or a letter as if from us, to the effect that the day of the Lord has come. ³ Let no one in any way deceive you, for *it will not come* unless the apostasy comes first, and the man of lawlessness is revealed, the son of destruction, ⁴who opposes and exalts himself above every so-called god or object of worship, so that he takes his seat in the temple of God, displaying himself as being God. ⁵ Do you not remember that while I was still with you, I was telling you these things? ⁶ And you know what restrains him now, so that in his time he will be revealed. ⁷ For the mystery of lawlessness is already at work; only he who now restrains *will do so* until he is taken out of the way. ⁸Then that lawless one will be revealed whom the Lord will slay with the breath of His mouth and bring to an end by the appearance of His coming; ⁹ *that is*, the one whose coming is in accord with the activity of Satan, with all power and signs and false wonders, ¹⁰ and with all the deception of wickedness for those who perish, because they did not receive the love of the truth so as to be saved. ¹¹ For this reason God will send upon them a deluding influence so that they will believe what is false, ¹² in order that they all may be judged who did not believe the truth, but took pleasure in wickedness. [13] But we should always give thanks to God for you, brethren beloved by the Lord, because God has chosen you from the beginning for salvation through sanctification by the Spirit and faith in the truth. [14] It was for this He called you through our gospel, that you may gain the glory of our Lord Jesus Christ. [15] So then, brethren, stand firm and hold to the traditions which you were taught, whether by word *of mouth* or by letter from us. [16] Now may our Lord Jesus Christ Himself and God our Father, who has loved us and given us eternal comfort and good hope by grace, [17]comfort and strengthen your hearts in every good work and word." (2 Thessalonians 2:1-17)

PRAYER: "Our Father, as we begin learning about the truth of this chapter and applying it to our lives help us to hear what Your Holy Spirit is speaking to us today and the days ahead. As we did at the beginning of chapter one, again we ask You to open our eyes to see the truth You have for us to see in this chapter. Open our minds to comprehend Your instruction for us. Open our hearts to commit our lives afresh to You in complete obedience to everything we learn here. We ask these things through our Lord and Savior, Jesus Christ. Amen."

DAY EIGHTEEN: "Apprehensive About the Future."

"[1]Now we request you, brethren, with regard to the coming of our Lord Jesus Christ and our gathering together to Him, [2]that you not be quickly shaken from your composure or be disturbed either by a spirit or a message or a letter as if from us, to the effect that the day of the Lord has come." (2:1-2)

Let's identify the obvious truths of this passage. Paul was writing about the Second Coming of Jesus. The Second Coming of Jesus will involve the gathering of Christians to Christ. Paul called this event the Day of the Lord. This truth was meant to be a source of comfort for the Thessalonian church (1 Thessalonians 4:16-18). However, due to some false teaching and messages, these folks were led to believe the Second Coming had already happened. This belief caused them to be apprehensive about the future. Paul's goal here was to set the record straight concerning these ideas.

This same kind of thing has happened over and over in our time. Apocalyptic prognosticators read disaster into every news headline. Some are overtaken by a spirit of gloom and doom. The books that are written from a negative stance flood the bookstores and are frequently bestsellers. As they are often proved wrong in their crystal ball theories, they simply readjust their predictions and write another bestseller. Unfortunately, gloom and doom sells.

We understand biblically that the future is not all full of flower petals falling from the heavens and immediate utopia. However, the scripture clearly teaches an eschatology of victory. The believer has suffered throughout church history. Pain, suffering, and hardship are a real part of this life on this fallen planet. But that is not the whole story.

Believers are empowered by the victory of Jesus to overcome evil. Believers have spiritual weapons and must use them in faith. There are many victories in the future for the church triumphant. Let us tell the whole story of Scripture, not just an emphasis on the gloom and doom part. Let's be encouraged by the whole truth about the end. Receive comfort and hope as we take note of the final statement of Paul in this chapter. "**16 Now may our Lord Jesus Christ Himself and God our Father, who has loved us and given us eternal comfort and good hope by grace, 17comfort and strengthen your hearts in every good work and word.**" (vs. 16-17)

CLOSING WORD: "**10 I heard a loud voice in heaven, saying, "Now the salvation, the power, and the Kingdom of our God, and the authority of his Christ has come; for the accuser of our brothers has been thrown** down, who accuses them before our God day and night. [11] They overcame him because of the Lamb's blood, and because of the word of their testimony. They didn't love their life, even to death. [12] Therefore rejoice, heavens, and you who dwell in them. Woe to the earth and to the sea, because the devil has gone down to you, having great wrath, knowing that he has but a short time." (Revelation 12:10-12)

PRAYER: "Father, as humans we often struggle with proper balance. We easily run off track on one side or the other. Help me to understand that I may endure many hard times in my life just as believers have throughout history. Also, help me to see the victory of Christ and to declare His triumph with great faith. Give me a testimony that is full of victory knowing that the time is short. Help me to overcome with the blood of Jesus and the word of my testimony unto death. Amen."

DAY NINETEEN: "Apostasy."

"Let no one in any way deceive you, for *it will not come* unless the apostasy comes first, and the man of lawlessness is revealed, the son of destruction." (2:3)

Again, let's look at what is obvious first. The Day of the Lord will not come unless two things occur prior: First, the Apostasy; Second, the Revelation of the Man of Lawlessness. Today we will look at the first part of this, the Apostasy. Remember, our theme in this chapter is *Awareness*.

These believers are told not to let anyone deceive them about this by any means, a letter, a message, a prophetic insight, or whatever means. Guarding themselves against deception is one of their main points of instruction here. It should be ours too.

Also, teaching about keeping the temple pure was a theme of Paul's, which he spoke about in an earlier passage in his previous letter immediately prior to his expose of the Second Coming (1

Thessalonians 4:3-8). The deceivers like to get the people of God to compromise the purity of their minds and bodies as they pollute the purity of doctrine (Revelation 2:14-17).

An apostasy here means, "falling away, rebellion." It is not to be translated as a "taken away" as some promoting a preconceived interpretation suggest translating it. That is not the meaning of the word here. The Thessalonians were instructed to guard themselves against deception, and a "falling away" is going to occur. Apostasy means, "falling away from the faith." It is a rebellion against the truth. Jesus predicted coming deceivers and deception in the context of the end of time (Matthew 24:10-13).

The falling away is not the falling away of the remnant church. In the same manner as all Israel was not the true Israel, but only the remnant were, all who are called Christians are not the true remnant of believers at the end of time. Can you see the parallel between Christ's first coming and His final coming in this regard?

This apostasy of nominal Christianity will become more and more prevalent in the final days of time. Those who have a mere form of godliness will give themselves over to seducing spirits and doctrines of devils. Those who had never adhered to real Christianity are going to abandon it all together finally. They had never really been changed by it but only knew it in a form. On the surface, it will be quite noticeable that large groups of professing believers no longer hold to the foundational truths of the gospel. This is referring to an open and widespread rebellion against the faith (1 Timothy 4:1).

CLOSING WORD: "**³ As he sat on the Mount of Olives, the disciples came to him privately, saying, "Tell us, when will these things be? What is the sign of your coming, and of the end of the age?" ⁴ Jesus answered them, "Be careful that no one leads you astray. ⁵ For many will come in my name, saying, 'I am the Christ,' and will lead many astray."** (Matthew 24:3-5)

PRAYER: "Holy Father, I am kept by Your saving and keeping power. Help me to stay alert to the times and guard myself and others against deception. Cause me to love You and Your truth. In Jesus' Name, I ask this, Amen."

DAY TWENTY: "Anarchy."

"Let no one in any way deceive you, for *it will not come* unless the apostasy comes first, and the man of lawlessness is revealed, the son of destruction." (2:3)

Let's look now at the second part of this warning. It is the Revelation of the Man of Lawlessness. He is the leader of the Apostasy we considered in Day Nineteen. He is lawless because he will openly oppose God's law. Lawlessness is so much of what he is about that it becomes his very title here. His end is destruction.

This verse doesn't necessarily call this man the Antichrist. He is lawless and opposes Christ. He proclaims himself to be God. He produces lying signs and wonders. He is involved with the place of worship. He is against Christians, therefore against Christ. Thus, in this sense, it is safe to consider him antichristian and the Antichrist (Daniel 8:10-13, 11:29-36, Revelation 11:1-7, 13:6).

This guy is the head of a movement that has existed throughout the history of the Church. The true believers have always been plagued with an antichristian opposition in one form or the other, whether from the government or false religious leaders. Believers have been troubled and persecuted because of this. There have been many antichrists (1 John 2:18). Also, believers have overcome this in every age. However, this text appears to put a final face on this accompanied with one last defeat of it. This is the capstone at the final peak of history and the triumph of good over evil.

The Man of Lawlessness is a real man. There is no other way to interpret this chapter faithfully given all of the personal references given here. He is a real eschatological person. This means he belongs to what we call the "end times." He is connected with the time when Christ returns (2:8). This has not occurred yet, as Christ has not returned in this manner (Acts 1:11).

CLOSING WORD: "**⁷ For many deceivers have gone out into the world, those who don't confess that Jesus Christ came in the flesh. This is the deceiver and the Antichrist. ⁸ Watch yourselves, that we don't lose the things which we have accomplished, but that we receive a full reward. ⁹ Whoever transgresses and doesn't remain in the teaching of Christ, doesn't have God. He who remains in the teaching, the same has both the Father and the Son. ¹⁰ If anyone comes to you, and doesn't bring this teaching, don't receive him into your house, and don't welcome him, ¹¹ for he who welcomes him participates in his evil deeds.**" (2 John 7-10)

PRAYER: "O Lord, You are the Christ. Guard us from evil and from the Antichrist in whatever form we face him. Strengthen us to overcome evil using the weapons You have given us to resist it. Mostly, guard us against deception, rebellion, and lawlessness that we may receive our full reward when we stand before Your throne on the last day. Amen."

DAY TWENTY-ONE: "Above Everything."

"**...who opposes and exalts himself above every so-called god or object of worship, so that he takes his seat in the temple of God, displaying himself as being God.**" (2:4)

The only other explanation than the above as I have given is to say the Man of Lawlessness is Herod. But this requires too many other interpretive applications that just don't fit the context. Remember, in this chapter the setting is the Second Coming of Jesus. Therefore, let us proceed on the path we are on with this text and see what else is there.

The Man of Lawlessness opposes God and exalts himself. This is rebellion and pride. He is self-centeredness personified. He desires the worship of humankind. In his arrogance, he pushes his agenda and himself into the very temple of God. Since he is lawless, he opposes God as God is the supreme law-giver. In his rebellion, he displays himself as being God.

The word used here for the *temple* is not the word one would use to describe the entire temple complex. It is the word for the sanctuary. For me, this can only have a reference in the New Covenant for the Church, the true Temple of God (1 Corinthians 3:16). That's how Paul used that word in his writings.

The Jewish Temple was a house left desolate. The final sacrifice for sin God recognized was Jesus, the Lamb of God. The Temple in the New Testament is the Christian Church. The coming end-of-time Man of Lawlessness will sit in the Temple of God and display himself as God. What can this mean?

If the Temple is used metaphorically, as it clearly is in Paul's letters, then the "seat" of the Man of Lawlessness is likely not literal. It must mean there will be a direct spiritual opposition to the people of God in the final days. This is consistent with other New Testament passages as well (Revelation 20:1-3, 7-10).

There is certainly much we do not know here so let's work with what we have in this verse. The Lawless One seeks worship by sitting in the place of worship and displaying himself as God. Paul warns them against being deceived. Paul warned them that this Lawless One would sit in the Temple.

Having a seat can mean different things (Matthew 23:2, 26:64, Acts 2:30-36). It doesn't have to be literal (Psalm 1:1, Revelation 2:13, 3:21). It can mean he has a place of authority or at least influence (Revelation 14:14-15, 20:4). Either way, he is connected in such a way as to have an influence on the worship.

He will be in the very midst of the church, as he has been in spirit throughout the church age. But this text gives him more influence and power than the "spirit of antichrist" dealt with by the earlier church. According to this text, he will have a seat.

His self-exaltation, claiming himself to be God makes him the ultimate humanist. As the philosophy of self-centeredness increases in many churches, it is not a stretch to see his influence become more and more predominant as time moves forward.

CLOSING WORD: **"Beloved, don't believe every spirit, but test the spirits, whether they are of God, because many false prophets have gone out into the world. 2 By this you know the Spirit of God: every spirit who confesses that Jesus Christ has come in the flesh is of God, 3 and every spirit who doesn't confess that Jesus Christ has come in the flesh is not of God, and this is the spirit of the Antichrist, of whom you have heard that it comes. Now it is in the world already. 4 You are of God, little children, and have overcome them; because greater is he who is in you than he who is in the world. 5 They are of the world. Therefore they speak of the world, and the world hears them. 6 We are of God. He who knows God listens to us. He who is not of God doesn't listen to us. By this we know the spirit of truth, and the spirit of error."** (1 John 4:16)

PRAYER: "Father, thank You for leading me into the path of truth. I ask that You will continually keep me from deception. Guard my heart against rebellion and pride. Help me to love Your law. Cause the Greater One who is in me to triumph over the Lawless One who is in the world. In the name of Jesus, I ask this. Amen."

DAY TWENTY-TWO: "Amnesia."

"Do you not remember that while I was still with you, I was telling you these things?" (2:5)

Paul had already taught these believers these things. However, much of what he taught them had been twisted around to the point he had to write these letters to help them unravel the tangled up message. He had to correct them.

We function in a "live and let live" society today in America. "Let others believe what they want," we say. "Mind your own business." However, Paul took the time to untangle faithfully the twisted up ideas that didn't represent the truth. He did this often. Therefore, Paul reminded them of what he had earlier taught them about these things.

He reminded them that there must be the Rebellion (Apostasy) and the revealing of the Lawless One prior to the coming of the Day of the Lord. Anyone who would tell them differently, by any other means (including a prophetic utterance) was not telling them the truth. His message hadn't changed.

Today, our country and many professing believers are suffering from rebellion, lawlessness, and a form of spiritual amnesia. Due to the recent overstretch of the United States Supreme redefining marriage many liberal mainstream churches will gleefully perform same-sex unions in the name of Christ. This is a rebellion against the Law of God. This is lawlessness in the sense of trying to supersede God's established law.

Another movement in recent years has worked to join Christianity and Islam. These are opposites in many ways. They are not compatible. We have forgotten our roots as a country, based on the principles of God's Word.

We have short term memory loss too. We can't even remember who attacked our country and killed thousands of innocent citizens on September 11, 2001. Many of our leaders want to be friends with terrorists. "May God help us not to forget what had made us a great country."

CLOSING WORD: "'This is now, beloved, the second letter that I have written to you; and in both of them I stir up your sincere mind by reminding you; ² that you should remember the words which were spoken before by the holy prophets, and the commandments of us, the apostles of the Lord and Savior: ³ knowing this first, that in the last days mockers will come, walking after their own lusts, ⁴ and saying, "Where is the promise of his coming? For, from the day that the fathers fell asleep, all things continue as they were from the beginning of the creation."' (2 Peter 3:1-4)

PRAYER: "Father, please give me a pure mind. Stir up my pure mind to remember every promise and every truth that You have given me to believe and pattern my life after. Give me a desire to read Your Word and adjust my mind and life to it. Amen."

DAY TWENTY-THREE: "Already at Work."

"⁶And you know what restrains him now, so that in his time he will be revealed. ⁷ For the mystery of lawlessness is already at work; only he who now restrains *will do so* until he is taken out of the way." (2:6-7)

Paul had apparently told these believers what was restraining the Lawless One from being revealed. The mystery of lawlessness was already at work even then. But it was being restrained from being fully manifested.

Even though the Man of Lawlessness hadn't come in his full manifestation, the spirit of lawlessness was still able to deceive those who did not love the truth (2 Thessalonians 2:9-12). This must be what John had warned about, emphasizing the "spirit of antichrist." He is restrained to operate spiritually, but will be able to come on the scene more directly and fully during the period of the very end of time (Revelation 20:3, 7-9).

There are many suggestions for who or what the restrainer is to which Paul referred. Due to space limitations, I will offer only a few thoughts. I cannot insist on any view.

First, it makes sense to me that God uses human government to restrain evil in the world. Paul says that human governmental leaders are used as God's ministers (Romans 13:1-7). If God lifted His influence on all human leaders (as He likely has done before in a measure in some instances at times throughout the history of humanity), worldwide chaos would undoubtedly occur.

Another reasonable way to identify the restrainer is as those who preach and teach the truth of the gospel. Paul could have been referring to himself and those who would later teach what he had. This is what Paul was doing in these letters. Like Daniel of old, Paul understood the mysteries (Daniel 2:47). Paul was restraining evil with the truth. Believers are salt in the earth and the light of the world. Those who proclaim the truth over and against the corruption and darkness are they who restrain evil by God's truth.

Revelation chapter twenty gives us a visual of the entire concept of this chapter. From the time Jesus ascended into heaven until He comes again, Satan is bound. An angel bound him. We are told in Revelation 20 that Satan does not have the power to deceive the nations until he is released for a little while at the end of the age. While he is bound, any person who *wants to* believe in God is not powerless to do it. Believers were authorized by Jesus and instructed to preach the gospel throughout the entire world. Of course, many are still deceived as they don't really love the truth (they don't *want to* believe). But anyone who wants to believe can. This text gives us a picture of restraint on the evil and a lifting of it (in his time) at the end of time before the final Judgment Day. "**...and you know what restrains him now, so that in his time he will be revealed.**"

Also, notice the connection of an angel with Revelation 20 and other passages concerning the end-time. Remember in the book of

Daniel the angels warring in the heavens (Daniel 10:13, 20-21). The first thing we see as Jesus ascended into heaven is an angel giving assurance of His return, although they don't know the time (Mark 13:32, Acts 1:11). Earlier in this letter, Paul mentioned the role of angels directly referring to the Second Coming of Jesus (1:7). Perhaps, God is using an angel to restrain the full manifestation of the Antichrist until "the time" He has chosen.

CLOSING WORD: "**[13] I command you before God, who gives life to all things, and before Christ Jesus, who before Pontius Pilate testified the good confession, [14] that you keep the commandment without spot, blameless, until the appearing of our Lord Jesus Christ; [15] which in its own times he will show, who is the blessed and only Ruler, the King of kings, and Lord of lords;...**" (1 Timothy 6:13-15)

PRAYER: "Dear Father, thank You for restraining evil at this time. Help me to follow You faithfully and resist the spirit of antichrist that is already at work. Keep me in the truth and from deception. Help me to trust Your timing for all things. In Jesus' name, Amen."

DAY TWENTY-FOUR: "Antichrist."

"**Then that lawless one will be revealed whom the Lord will slay with the breath of His mouth and bring to an end by the appearance of His coming;...**" (2:8)

Let's keep the timeline in mind. "Then" is a word dealing with timing. Paul said the Lawless One would be revealed during this timeframe of these other events. All of these signs are in the timeframe of the Lord's return. That's one reason I don't follow the interpretation that the Man of Lawlessness is Herod and that this is all already fulfilled. The timing of this passage above directly relates to the return of Christ at the end of time. Putting this alongside Revelation 20, this is during the final days when Satan is loosed for a season to deceive the nations for a final time.

Who is Antichrist? According to the Apostle John he is one who denies that Jesus is the Christ (e.g., as the Messiah and as God in the flesh), denies both the Father and the Son (e.g., the Trinity), refuses to confess the truth about Jesus Christ, and operates with deception (1 John 2:22-23, 4:3 and 2 John 7). All of this directly relates to apostasy.

There are and have been many who are antichrist according to these guidelines (1 John 2:18). But Paul is more direct here. He is more personal above in verse eight of Second Thessalonians. Paul is speaking of a specific man appearing in the time period before the return of Jesus.

CLOSING WORD: "**[18] Little children, these are the end times, and as you heard that the Antichrist is coming, even now many antichrists have arisen. By this we know that it is the final hour. [19] They went out from us, but they didn't belong to us; for if they had belonged to us, they would have continued with us. But they left, that they might be revealed that none of them belong to us. [20] You have an anointing from the Holy One, and you all have knowledge. [21] I have not written to you because you don't know the truth, but because you know it, and because no lie is of the truth. [22] Who is the liar but he who denies that Jesus is the Christ? This is the Antichrist, he who denies the Father and the Son. [23] Whoever denies the Son, the same doesn't have the Father. He who confesses the Son has the Father also.**" (1 John 2:18-23)

PRAYER: "Our Father, thank You for the truth given to us in Your Word. Thank You for the anointing of Your Holy Spirit that keeps me from following the lie. I confess Your name, Father, and I acknowledge Jesus is the Christ, the Son of the living God. I deny and resist the spirit of antichrist. I bow my knee before You and willingly declare that Jesus is Lord to the glory of God the Father. Amen."

DAY TWENTY-FIVE: "Appearance."

"Then that lawless one will be revealed whom the Lord will slay with the breath of His mouth and bring to an end by the appearance of His coming;..." (2:8)

The lawless one will be revealed. Therefore, we can say that it likely hasn't happened given the specifics Paul described here. I believe he will operate within the framework given in this chapter and illustrated in the Book of Revelation for a short time. We should watch and pray and be ready for our Lord's return. If we are doing this, it is not probable that we will not recognize the apostasy, the rebellion, and revealing of this character as these events occur if they happen in our lifetime.

The revelation of the Lawless One is to bring him to judgment. When the Lord Jesus returns in glory He will execute judgment upon him and bring history to an end (Revelation 1:7, 16). This is evident from this chapter and Revelation 19:11-21 where, in symbolic language the beast and the false prophet suffer their final defeat. Revelation 20:7-10 reiterates this including the judgment upon Satan, the one whom they loved, worshiped, and served. Even so, come, Lord Jesus.

Notice also, that the victory of Jesus in verse eight above and in the Revelation text below uses very strong imagery. Therefore, it is not reasonable to conclude that this is referring to a physical battle. In keeping with our theme of *awareness* and with the topic of the believers not being deceived, we should prepare our hearts and minds for spiritual warfare in the end-times (2 Corinthians 10:4, Ephesians 6:10-20, Revelation 12:10-12). An intense, widespread rebellion and apostasy indicates a major spiritual battle.

CLOSING WORD: **"¹¹ I saw the heaven opened, and behold, a white horse, and he who sat on it is called Faithful and True. In** righteousness he judges and makes war. ¹²His eyes are a flame of fire, and on his head are many crowns. He has names written and a name written which no one knows but he himself. ¹³He is clothed in a garment sprinkled with blood. His name is called "The Word of God." ¹⁴The armies which are in heaven followed him on white horses, clothed in white, pure, fine linen. ¹⁵Out of his mouth proceeds a sharp, double-edged sword, that with it he should strike the nations. He will rule them with an iron rod. He treads the wine press of the fierceness of the wrath of God, the Almighty. ¹⁶He has on his garment and on his thigh a name written, "KING OF KINGS, AND LORD OF LORDS." ¹⁷I saw an angel standing in the sun. He cried with a loud voice, saying to all the birds that fly in the sky, "Come! Be gathered together to the great supper of God, ¹⁸that you may eat the flesh of kings, the flesh of captains, the flesh of mighty men, and the flesh of horses and of those who sit on them, and the flesh of all men, both free and slave, and small and great." ¹⁹I saw the beast, and the kings of the earth, and their armies, gathered together to make war against him who sat on the horse, and against his army. ²⁰The beast was taken, and with him the false prophet who worked the signs in his sight, with which he deceived those who had received the mark of the beast and those who worshiped his image. These two were thrown alive into the lake of fire that burns with sulfur." (Revelation 19:11-20)

PRAYER: "I know You have a plan for the ages, O Lord. May evil be judged by You, the Righteous One. Come, O Lord, that we may see You in Your glory and worship before Your throne throughout eternity. Amen."

DAY TWENTY-SIX: "Activity of Satan."

"*...that is*, the one whose coming is in accord with the activity of Satan, with all power and signs and false wonders,..." (2:9)

I expect more Satanic activity as we get closer and closer to the end of history. I think this activity is directly connected with deception and the Apostasy. Believers must cling to the truth and not to signs and wonders. This doesn't mean that we don't believe that God can and does work signs in the world. But the sign isn't the most important thing. The truth is. The key here is never to reject the truth. Ask God to give you and your family and friends a great love for the truth.

When considering these things, I can't help but picture in my mind Moses standing before Pharaoh and his magicians. They could perform many signs. However, God worked signs through Moses also. He also worked many signs in the Early Church. I believe we can trust Him to do the same in our time as it may be needed.

CLOSING WORD: "**[23]Then if any man tells you, 'Behold, here is the Christ,' or, 'There,' don't believe it. [24] For there will arise false christs, and false prophets, and they will show great signs and wonders, so as to lead astray, if possible, even the chosen ones.**" (Matthew 24:23-24)

PRAYER: "Lord Jesus, help me not to follow after every sign and wonder I see, but to judge all things according to Your Word. Give me the discernment I need to determine what is Your Spirit and what is the deceiver. I ask this in Jesus' name. Amen."

DAY TWENTY-SEVEN: "All the Deception."

"**...and with all the deception of wickedness for those who perish, because they did not receive the love of the truth so as to be saved.**" (2:10)

Rebellion is sinful. Sometimes folks are proud of being rebellious. This is a foolish attitude and dangerous behavior. We should want to submit to God and our godly leaders. We open ourselves up for deception when we do not (Hebrews 13:7, 1 Peter 5:6-11).

Our keyword for this chapter is *awareness*. Our world is ripe with deceivers and deception. Folks in the church world are eager to believe practically any new philosophy that comes down the pike. For many, the thought of judging between what is true and what is not is an offensive idea. Therefore, many folks swallow any teaching they are fed. It will only get worse along these lines as the end of all things draws nearer. Let us be those who read our Bible and prove what is true and good.

CLOSING WORD: "**Test all things, and hold firmly that which is good.**" (1 Thessalonians 5:21)

PRAYER: "Lord Jesus, help me not to believe everything I hear, even from those who claim to be religious. Guide me to prove all things and to hold firmly to that which is good. I ask this in Jesus' name. Amen."

DAY TWENTY-EIGHT: "Agape of the Truth."

"**...and with all the deception of wickedness for those who perish, because they did not receive the love of the truth so as to be saved.**" (2:10)

Here is the key. The wicked are deceived because they do not have a love for the truth. Let us check ourselves in this regard. Let us ask God to give us the right attitude and motive.

We cannot be saved without loving what God loves and hating what God hates (1 John 2:15-17). Jesus is the truth personified. If we truly love Him, we will love His Word. If we are offended at the truth of His Word, we are offended with Jesus. Let us repent at our offense with the truth and ask God to save us according to the truth. This is the only Biblical way to be saved.

CLOSING WORD: "**Jesus said to him, "I am the way, the truth, and the life. No one comes to the Father, except through me.**" (John 14:6)

PRAYER: "Lord Jesus, I come to You now. You are the way, the truth, and the life. Make me into a lover of truth. I submit myself and my life to Your way and truth. I resist the lie of the deceiver, the flesh, and the world. Sanctify me by Your truth today. In Your name, I ask this. Amen."

DAY TWENTY-NINE: "A Deluding Influence."

"[11]**For this reason God will send upon them a deluding influence so that they will believe what is false, [12] in order that they all may be judged who did not believe the truth, but took pleasure in wickedness.**" (2:11-12)

God is serious about the truth. He is serious about sin. Often His judgment is to allow us to have what we want (Roman 1:26). The deluding influence here appears to be just that. They will love wickedness and despise the truth. Therefore, God will let them have what they want.

What would happen in the world if God lifted His restraint upon evil? In this text, it's as if He will remove His hand of restraint upon the people of that day. Imagine the world without God specifically keeping evil in check. Imagine the evil hearts and corrupt minds operating without a governor. Sin and evil would be accelerated. Except God limit the time, who could survive?

He gave Pharaoh the opportunity to cooperate. After a certain point, He hardened Pharaoh in his resolve to rebel. Then Pharaoh was obsessed with killing the chosen people. His restraint was gone. God gave him up to his obsession.

Every believer should check themselves on what gives them pleasure (Psalm 16:11). Do you still take great pleasure in hearing and reading His holy Word? Do you still enjoy praying and fellowshipping with Him? Do you still want to spend time in His presence and with other believers?

CLOSING WORD: "[20] **For the invisible things of him since the creation** of the world are clearly seen, being perceived through the things that are made, even his everlasting power and divinity; that they may be without excuse. ²¹ Because, knowing God, they didn't glorify him as God, neither gave thanks, but became vain in their reasoning, and their senseless heart was darkened. ²² Professing themselves to be wise, they became fools, ²³ and traded the glory of the incorruptible God for the likeness of an image of corruptible man, and of birds, and four-footed animals, and creeping things. ²⁴ Therefore God also gave them up in the lusts of their hearts to uncleanness, that their bodies should be dishonored among themselves, ²⁵ who exchanged the truth of God for a lie, and worshiped and served the creature rather than the Creator, who is blessed forever. Amen." (Romans 1:20-25)

PRAYER: "Search me, O Lord. Remove any evil thing that I may be holding onto. Cleanse my heart and mind and make me love Your truth. Create in me a clean heart and renew a righteous spirit within me. In Your holy name, I ask this. Amen."

DAY THIRTY: "Always Give Thanks."

"But we should always give thanks to God for you, brethren beloved by the Lord, because God has chosen you from the beginning for salvation through sanctification by the Spirit and faith in the truth." (2:13)

Let us be thankful to God for our brothers and sisters in Christ. Fellowship with other believers is essential for healthy Christian living. If times get tough, we need to be there for one another (Acts 4:32-37).

The saved are believers because of God's great love and election (Deuteronomy 7:6-8). The evidence of salvation is sanctification by the Holy Spirit and faith in the truth. The saved take pleasure in doing good works. The unbeliever takes pleasure in wickedness. Let us all examine ourselves in this regard (2 Corinthians 13:5).

The explanation of salvation here is through sanctification by the Spirit and faith in the truth. These believers should be able to contrast their desire for holiness and their love for the truth with those who take pleasure in wickedness. We should be able to do the same.

CLOSING WORD: "**9 Or don't you know that the unrighteous will not inherit God's Kingdom? Don't be deceived. Neither the sexually immoral, nor idolaters, nor adulterers, nor male prostitutes, nor homosexuals, 10 nor thieves, nor covetous, nor drunkards, nor slanderers, nor extortionists, will inherit God's Kingdom. 11 Such were some of you, but you were washed. But you were sanctified. But you were justified in the name of the Lord Jesus, and in the Spirit of our God.**" (1 Corinthians 6:9-11)

PRAYER: "Thank You Lord for saving my soul. Thank You for giving me the desire to live right. Thank You for giving me Your Holy Spirit to help me to worship and serve You. Work Your righteousness into my life every day. I am Yours, O Lord God. Amen."

DAY THIRTY-ONE: "Answering the Call."

"**It was for this He called you through our gospel, that you may gain the glory of our Lord Jesus Christ.**" (2:14)

Salvation results from responding to the call of God. The gospel gives us the framework to answer to this call. The purpose is for us to give glory to God. God gets the glory since He chose us for salvation. Jesus gets the glory since He died to redeem us. The Holy Spirit is gloried as Lord and life-giver since He empowers us to love God and follow Jesus. Our salvation is all to the glory of God.

If it were not for His calling and electing us to salvation, we would be deceived like the rest of the world. But thanks be to God, He has saved us from the deception of the Devil, the Antichrist, and the False Prophet. Now we live our lives in such a way as to bring glory to God's holy name. Let us praise Him and be thankful for this.

CLOSING WORD: "³ **Blessed be the God and Father of our Lord Jesus Christ, who has blessed us with every spiritual blessing in the heavenly places in Christ; ⁴ even as he chose us in him before the foundation of the world, that we would be holy and without defect before him in love; ⁵ having predestined us for adoption as children through Jesus Christ to himself, according to the good pleasure of his desire, ⁶ to the praise of the glory of his grace, by which he freely gave us favor in the Beloved,…**" (Ephesians 1:3-6)

PRAYER: "Heavenly Father, I recognize that I am saved today because of You chose me to be Your child. O how thankful I am for this. It is all of grace. You alone receive the glory for my salvation. I resolve to live in such a way as to bring glory to Your name in the earth. Amen."

DAY THIRTY-TWO: "Affirming the Traditions."

"**So then, brethren, stand firm and hold to the traditions which you were taught, whether by word *of mouth* or by letter from us.**" (2:15)

The old preacher said, "You must stand for something or you will fall for anything." Here's the instruction from Paul, "Stand firm and hold to the traditions." God would not tell them to stand firm if they could not do it. We can also stand firm also. We must resolve to stand in our day as the New Testament believers were instructed to (Ephesians 6:11-14).

For many, the word "tradition" is a bad word. Admittedly, some traditions are useless. But we must not throw out the baby with the bath water. Some traditions are good and should be held onto. It all depends on what the tradition is founded on.

The traditions here are the teachings of Paul. The New Testament had not yet been completed. Therefore, the teachings of Paul were either by word or by letter. He instructed them to hold firmly to these teachings. Let us do the same.

CLOSING WORD: "**Watch! Stand firm in the faith! Be courageous! Be strong!**" (1 Corinthians 16:13)

PRAYER: "Father, I ask You to help me to stand for what I should stand for and to not be distracted by other things. Help me to see what is needed, and to be courageous for the Kingdom of God. In Jesus' name I pray. Amen."

DAY THIRTY-THREE: "All Good Work and Word."

"**[16]Now may our Lord Jesus Christ Himself and God our Father, who has loved us and given us eternal comfort and good hope by grace, [17]comfort and strengthen your hearts in every good work and word.**" (2:16-17)

The goal of the Christian life here is to produce good works and words by the grace of God. For this, we need our hearts comforted in the face of an evil world and antichrist system. We need strength to do the will of God. Paul declares this over these saints. Let us declare this over ourselves and every other believer we know.

We need hope in a hopeless world. We have a good hope by grace. God has flooded our hearts and minds with His grace and good hope. Let us be so full of hope that others ask us about it. That's a good testimony to have.

CLOSING WORD: "**[15] But sanctify the Lord God in your hearts; and always be ready to give an answer to everyone who asks you a reason concerning the hope that is in you, with humility and fear: [16] having a good conscience; that, while you are spoken against as evildoers, they may be disappointed who curse your good way of life in Christ.**" (1 Peter 3:15-16)

PRAYER: "Dear Lord, keep my heart and mind focused on You and Your kingdom that I may have a good conscience. Make me aware of the evil around me that I may stand against it according to Your truth. Lead me to speak blessings over Your children. Cause me to declare hope into hopeless situations. Make me a vessel fit for Your use and worthy of the Kingdom. In the name of Jesus, the King. Amen."

DAY THIRTY-FOUR: "Affirmation and Action."

The power of God's Word is activated as we read, study, and meditate on it and the Holy Spirit makes it a reality in our lives by the grace of God. Let us ask God to search our hearts and help us to apply the truth of chapter two to our lives.

THE WORD FOR TODAY: **"⁷The law of the Lord *is* perfect, converting the soul; The testimony of the Lord *is* sure, making wise the simple; ⁸The statutes of the Lord *are* right, rejoicing the heart; The commandment of the Lord *is* pure, enlightening the eyes; ⁹The fear of the Lord *is* clean, enduring forever; The judgments of the Lord *are* true *and* righteous altogether. ¹⁰ More to be desired *are they* than gold, Yea, than much fine gold; Sweeter also than honey and the honeycomb. ¹¹ Moreover by them Your servant is warned, *and* in keeping them *there is* great reward. ¹² Who can understand *his* errors? Cleanse me from secret *faults*. ¹³ Keep back Your servant also from presumptuous *sins;* Let them not have dominion over me. Then I shall be blameless, and I shall be innocent of great transgression. ¹⁴ Let the words of my mouth and the meditation of my heart be acceptable in Your sight, O Lord, my strength and my Redeemer."** (Psalm 19:7-14, NKJV)

PRAYER: "Gracious Father, I come to You today thanking You that You have saved me and called me to follow You. I ask You now to reveal to me ways I can increase in understanding and operate in the calling You have for me in my life. Reveal the purpose of Your Kingdom in my time. Make me aware of the evil around me. Activate good hope within me and give me an answer to give to those who ask me about it. In Christ's name, I ask this. Amen."

THE WORD IN ACTION:

Identify the Kingdom truths God Has affirmed in you during this study of His Word:

_____
_____
_____
_____
_____
_____
_____
_____
_____
_____
_____
_____
_____
_____
_____
_____
_____
_____

Dear Father, please show me how You want to activate this truth in my daily life:

_____
_____
_____
_____
_____
_____
_____
_____
_____
_____
_____
_____
_____
_____
_____
_____
_____
_____

3

KINGDOM ADVICE

DAY THIRTY-FIVE: "Activation."

Today let's get familiar with chapter three of Second Thessalonians. In this chapter, after Paul requested the prayers of these believers he shared some important Kingdom Advice to strengthen them in their faith. Then he offered several practical guidelines about daily life. I am confident we will uncover some encouraging words and useful advice from reading this chapter carefully and applying it to our lives. Let's make this our goal as we go forward with chapter three now.

CLOSING WORD: "[1]Finally, brethren, pray for us that the word of the Lord will spread rapidly and be glorified, just as *it did* also with you; [2]and that we will be rescued from perverse and evil men; for not all have faith. [3] But the Lord is faithful, and He will strengthen and protect you from the evil *one*. [4] We have confidence in the Lord concerning you, that you are doing and will *continue to* do what we command. [5]May the Lord direct your hearts into the love of God and into the steadfastness of Christ. ⁶Now we command you, brethren, in the name of our Lord Jesus Christ, that you keep away from every brother who leads an unruly life and not according to the tradition which you received from us. ⁷ For you yourselves know how you ought to follow our example, because we did not act in an undisciplined manner among you, ⁸ nor did we eat anyone's bread without paying for it, but with labor and hardship we *kept* working night and day so that we would not be a burden to any of you; ⁹ not because we do not have the right *to this*, but in order to offer ourselves as a model for you, so that you would follow our example. ¹⁰For even when we were with you, we used to give you this order: if anyone is not willing to work, then he is not to eat, either. ¹¹ For we hear that some among you are leading an undisciplined life, doing no work at all, but acting like busybodies. ¹²Now such persons we command and exhort in the Lord Jesus Christ to work in quiet fashion and eat their own bread. ¹³ But as for you, brethren, do not grow weary of doing good. ¹⁴ If anyone does not obey our instruction in this letter, take special note of that person and do not associate with him, so that he will be put to shame. ¹⁵ *Yet* do not regard him as an enemy, but admonish him as a brother. ¹⁶ Now may the Lord of peace Himself continually grant you peace in every circumstance. The Lord be with you all! ¹⁷ I, Paul, write this greeting with my own hand, and this is a distinguishing mark in every letter; this is the way I write. ¹⁸ The grace of our Lord Jesus Christ be with you all." (2 Thessalonians 3:1-18)

PRAYER: "Our Father, as I begin learning the truth of this chapter and applying it to my life help me to hear what Your Holy Spirit is speaking to me from Your holy Word. I believe Your Word is alive and full of power. Therefore, again I ask You to open my eyes to see the truth You have for me to see in this passage. Open my mind to comprehend Your instruction to me. Open my heart to commit my life afresh to You in complete obedience to everything You reveal to me here. We ask these things through the Lord Jesus Christ. Amen."

DAY THIRTY-SIX: "Ask."

"Finally, brethren, pray for us that the word of the Lord will spread rapidly and be glorified, just as *it did* also with you;..." (3:1)

This verse reveals some keys ways in which the Kingdom of God advances in the earth. In this text, the Kingdom advances through proclamation and prayer. Jesus commanded the disciples to go into the world and proclaim the gospel. Paul believed prayer could enhance the success of spreading the Word. He often asked the saints to pray for him in this regard (Ephesians 6:19-20, Colossians 4:2-3). It is not enough to prepare to preach through study alone. The preacher needs to pray and have others pray for them. This is some good Kingdom Advice.

This verse applies to every believer. Every Christian is called to proclaim the truth in some manner. This passage shows us how to have more success in this area.

Bible believing saints should not assume that God will automatically call those He has elected unto salvation without our participation. The fact that we pray and proclaim is evidence that we are among the elect. The proof that God is calling a person to follow Him is that they respond to the gospel message in some way. We pray and proclaim because He has chosen us to salvation. Then He uses our prayer and preaching to call others unto repentance. It is all grace, and all glory goes unto God.

God can do anything. He has, however, chosen to do certain things by using us. Our prayer and proclamation of the gospel are a couple of the things He has chosen to use. Preaching accomplishes wonders. But let us remember that prayer is meant to accompany preaching. Therefore, let us pray and preach the gospel. Amen.

CLOSING WORD: **"For since, in the wisdom of God, the world through wisdom did not know God, it pleased God through the**

foolishness of the message preached to save those who believe." (1 Corinthians 1:21, NKJV)

PRAYER: "Father, I pray today for everyone who will preach Your Word today and this coming Sunday as those set apart to preach in this way. I also pray for every believer who preaches the gospel at every level, as we are all called to do. Give us boldness to proclaim the truth. Provide us with an understanding of the gospel and how to communicate it. Anoint us with Your Spirit and cause many souls to come to true repentance. Let Your Word and truth advance in our land and in our world speedily. I ask this in the name of Jesus Christ, the Savior. Amen."

DAY THIRTY-SEVEN: "And That We Will Be Rescued."

"...and that we will be rescued from perverse and evil men; for not all have faith." (3:2)

Paul also asked them to pray for him and his company for protection against perverse and evil men. He expected opposition. He didn't believe everybody was saved and had some inner spark that needed to be fanned. He stated explicitly that **"not all have faith."** That's not judging as many today would claim. It is merely stating the obvious.

Jesus said, **"You shall know them by their fruit"** (Matthew 7:15-20). It is not enough to claim a right relationship with God. Our lives must show the biblical fruit that is supposed to accompany our claims.

Paul asked for prayer to protect them from these opposing faithless men. They who oppose the gospel obviously do not have the fruit of faith and, therefore, expose themselves as faithless men. Paul believed that prayer would help their situation by giving protection against these evil men. Here he was taking the shield of faith for protection against the Devil's attacks (Ephesians 6:10-16). He asked for prayer for his endeavors, as he often did (Ephesians 6:18-20).

We should also expect opposition in our day. "...**for not all have faith.**" Therefore, we must pray for protection for ourselves and our sisters and brothers in Christ. Not everyone is happy when the gospel starts advancing in an area. Not everyone has faith. Not everyone is going to be saved. Therefore, we must pray for success against evil and ask God to give us fruit for our labors.

CLOSING WORD: "**[16]...and above all, taking the shield of faith, with which you will be able to extinguish all the fiery arrows of the evil one. [17] Take the helmet of salvation and the sword of the Spirit, which is the word of God. [18] Pray in the Spirit always with all kinds of prayer and supplication. To that end be alert with all perseverance and supplication for all the saints. [19] Pray for me, that the power to speak may be given to me, that I may open my mouth boldly to make known the mystery of the gospel, [20] for which I am an ambassador in chains, that I may speak boldly as I ought to speak.**" (Ephesians 6:16-20, MEV)

PRAYER: "Father, I ask You today to protect my sisters and brothers throughout the world who have faith. Keep them safe and protect them from harm. Help them to proclaim Your truth as we all should. Give us all success against the opposing forces of evil. O Lord, deliver us from evil, for Thine is the Kingdom, and the power, and the glory forever and ever. Let Your Word and truth advance speedily in our land and throughout the whole earth. I ask this in the name of Jesus Christ, the Deliverer and King of all the earth. Amen."

DAY THIRTY-EIGHT: "And He Will Strengthen."

"**But the Lord is faithful, and He will strengthen and protect you from the evil *one*.**" (3:3)

God is faithful even when we are not. We are safe because of Him, not because of us. He is the faithful, covenant-keeping God. We can trust that He will give us the strength we need. He will protect us from evil. Nothing can touch us without His permission. We are safe in His hands.

Often we want to be delivered out of our situation. Sometimes He does this. Sometimes He uses the situation as the means of delivering us to something better. However, His usual method is not to remove us from the situation but to preserve us within the situation and to strengthen us through it. We ask Him not to lead us into trial and temptation but to deliver us from the evil one when we pray the Lord's Prayer. He told us to pray in this way (Matthew 6:9-13).

Therefore, when we are going through a difficult time, we know He has a purpose for it (Romans 8:28). Otherwise, He would have removed it. So we must then ask Him for the strength to persevere in the difficult situation. He will give us the strength we need. Evil will not overcome God's people. He is faithful. Therefore, expect His strength to get you through the difficulty.

CLOSING WORD: "**[8] For we would not, brothers, have you ignorant of our troubles which came to us in Asia. We were pressured beyond measure, above strength, so that we despaired even of life. [9] We had the sentence of death in ourselves, so that we would not trust in ourselves, but in God who raises the dead. [10] He delivered us from so great a death and does deliver us. In Him we trust that He will still deliver us, [11] as you help together by praying for us, so that thanks may be given by many on our behalf for the gift bestowed upon us by means of many persons.**" (2 Corinthians 1:8-11)

PRAYER: "Father, today I again appeal to the prayer Your Son, Jesus taught us to pray when He said, "**[9]In this manner, therefore, pray: Our Father in heaven, Hallowed be Your name. [10]Your kingdom come. Your will be done On earth as** *it is* **in heaven. [11]Give us this day our daily bread. [12] And forgive us our debts, As we forgive our debtors. [13]And do not lead us into temptation, But deliver us from the evil one. For Yours** is the kingdom and the power and the glory forever. Amen" (Matt. 6:9-13).

DAY THIRTY-NINE: "Appreciation and Authority."

"We have confidence in the Lord concerning you, that you are doing and will *continue to* do what we command." (3:4)

Authority is a necessity for growth, stability, and security. It is a mess when it is not based on the right things. Spiritual authority is based on the mutual faith of believers in the Lord. He is Lord of all, including whom He puts into positions of authority. Spiritual authority is effective when it is based on faith and unity.

The peace of God causes us to continue to strive for unity. We are not at war with each other. We are at peace with God and each other. Rebellion is based on pride. Stubbornness reveals deeper issues within a person. Cooperation and submission reveal spiritual peace and godly purpose. Obedience to God and godly leaders prove that one is motivated by love and has overcome pride and self-centeredness.

It is a blessed situation when the people respect the leaders, and the leaders have confidence that the people are going to do the right thing. The entire body of Christ is strengthened to advance the Kingdom purposes when they can function as a unified body.

The authority of the leaders is based on the truth of the Word. However, it must be communicated in love to be truly effective and to last in a relationship. "May we all strive to appreciate each other and continue to submit to godly authority."

CLOSING WORD: **"[17]Obey your leaders and submit to them, for they watch on behalf of your souls, as those who will give account, that they may do this with joy, and not with groaning, for that would be unprofitable for you. [18] Pray for us, for we are persuaded that we have a good conscience, desiring to live honorably in all things. [19] I strongly** urge you to do this, that I may be restored to you sooner" (Hebrews 13:17-19).

PRAYER: "²⁰Now may the God of peace, who brought again from the dead the great shepherd of the sheep with the blood of an eternal covenant, our Lord Jesus, ²¹ make you complete in every good work to do his will, working in you that which is well pleasing in his sight, through Jesus Christ, to whom be the glory forever and ever. Amen" (Hebrews 13:20-21).

DAY FORTY: "Aiming for the Right Things."

"⁵May the Lord direct your hearts into the love of God and into the steadfastness of Christ." (3:5)

Without God directing our hearts, we would follow the flesh, the world, or the Evil One. But God leads us to go on the path He wants us to go. Often, protection from evil is a result of not going down the wrong path. This proper way is revealed to us as God directs our heart (Proverbs 16:9). He directs us "into the love of God and steadfastness of Christ." It works best when it begins in our heart by God and then works out in our actions.

Again, in the context of the entire letter, protection from deception would be involved here. We love God and, therefore, love the truth and are not easily deceived into going down the wrong path. God directs the heart of the believer when the believer is absorbed into the love of God. If we love God, we will do what He has said for us to do (John 14:15).

This requires steadfastness. Salvation is a walk, not just an experience or a prayer. We need to persevere in our faith. Christ in us is the hope of glory (Colossians 1:27). Christ in us causes us to endure hardship and be steadfast and unmovable (1 John 4:4). There is no doubt, this includes patience that comes from the expectation of Christ's return (2 Thessalonians 1:7, James 5:7-8). The believer knows Christ is in him and will return (Hebrews 10:37). This is a purifying hope (1 John 3:2-3).

CLOSING WORD: "**Therefore, my beloved brethren, be steadfast, immovable, always abounding in the work of the Lord, knowing that your toil is not *in* vain in the Lord.**" (1 Corinthians 15:58, NASB)

PRAYER: "Father, please direct my path. O Lord, lead me in the paths of righteousness for Your name's sake. Help me to walk in the love of God that is in my heart by the Holy Spirit. Make me steadfast and unmovable in the right areas. Complete Your work in me. In Jesus' name. Amen."

DAY FORTY-ONE: "Avoiding Trouble."

"**Now we command you, brethren, in the name of our Lord Jesus Christ, that you keep away from every brother who leads an unruly life and not according to the tradition which you received from us.**" (3:6)

Paul shared some important, practical, godly advice with these believers in this chapter. He began by emphasizing the connection between prayer with the advancing of God's Kingdom on earth. Then he turned to what may seem like even more practical advice.

The believer is called to be an example to the world around him and to one another. They are not to live unruly lives or be actively involved with those who do. Much trouble can be avoided by just staying clear of those whom you know are troublemakers. This is a part of God directing the path of the believer.

Part of this is from holding a deep value for the truth they had been taught. This is the doctrine of the Apostles, but it is also the practical teaching of how to live in this world. Paul had taught there is a right way to live. In the first letter, we called it: Worshiping, Working, and Waiting." Here we call it "Kingdom Advice." Paul was certainly deeply spiritual and theological. But he was also very practical. It is God's will for our theology to translate into our daily lives.

CLOSING WORD: "⁷Go from the presence of a foolish man, when you do not perceive *in him* the lips of knowledge. ⁸The wisdom of the prudent *is* to understand his way, but the folly of fools *is* deceit. ⁹Fools mock at sin, but among the upright *there is* favor. ¹⁰The heart knows its own bitterness, and a stranger does not share its joy. ¹¹The house of the wicked will be overthrown, but the tent of the upright will flourish. ¹²There is a way *that seems* right to a man, but its end *is* the way of death." (Proverbs 14:7-12)

PRAYER: "Father, help me to identify those whom You desire for me to be a witness to and those whom I should avoid. Let my light shine in darkness by the simple and honest way I live my life unto You. Amen."

DAY FORTY-TWO: "Acting Right."

"For you yourselves know how you ought to follow our example, because we did not act in an undisciplined manner among you,..." (3:7)

These leaders wanted the other believers to follow their example. Part of leadership is setting an example for others. This is a missing element in the modern American Christian Church. Lord, have mercy.

That doesn't mean leaders are to be soft and easy all of the time. Paul was an understanding leader but also tough. We need the grace of God to properly balance going too far in either direction.

Discipline is the root word of discipleship. Paul taught them that the grace of God teaches believers to live godly, disciplined lives (Titus 2:11-13). Today, many have redefined grace to mean everyone can sin as much as they want, and no one should judge anyone else. That's absurd. Godly people are called to live holy lives. Paul and his associates exhibited disciple and godliness to the Thessalonian

Church. "May God raise up disciplined leaders among us today! Amen."

CLOSING WORD: "¹²Therefore don't let sin reign in your mortal body, that you should obey it in its lusts. ¹³ Also, do not present your members to sin as instruments of unrighteousness, but present yourselves to God, as alive from the dead, and your members as instruments of righteousness to God. ¹⁴ For sin will not have dominion over you. For you are not under law, but under grace. ¹⁵ What then? Shall we sin, because we are not under law, but under grace? May it never be! ¹⁶ Don't you know that when you present yourselves as servants and obey someone, you are the servants of whomever you obey; whether of sin to death, or of obedience to righteousness? ¹⁷ But thanks be to God, that, whereas you were bondservants of sin, you became obedient from the heart to that form of teaching to which you were delivered. ¹⁸ Being made free from sin, you became bondservants of righteousness." (Romans 6:12-18)

PRAYER: "Father, I know I am often unruly and undisciplined in Your ways. My flesh always wants to go another direction. Teach me Your ways and guide me into proper Christian discipline that I may be Your disciple in word and deed. Amen."

DAY FORTY-THREE: "Anyone's Bread."

"⁸...nor did we eat anyone's bread without paying for it, but with labor and hardship we *kept* working night and day so that we would not be a burden to any of you; ⁹ not because we do not have the right *to this*, but in order to offer ourselves as a model for you, so that you would follow our example. ¹⁰For even when we were with you, we used to give you this order: if anyone is not willing to work, then he is not to eat, either." (3:8-10)

Working hard unto the Lord is a good testimony. Laziness is sinful. Again, we need discipline. The Apostles also set a great example in this area. They had the spiritual right to receive material compensation for their spiritual work among the Thessalonians. This was God's method in the Old Covenant and was carried on for the New Covenant (1 Corinthians 9:14). But Paul set a great example of work among these people not using his spiritual right in this area (1 Corinthians 9:11-12).

Paul honored work, as the Scripture does. God put Adam to work in the Garden of Eden before sin entered in. Adam used his creativity to shape his new world (Genesis 2:19-20). Part of the curse in the Garden was the change of the meaning of work and pleasure. After the Fall, instead of eating of the trees in the Garden man would have to work and sweat to get his food (Genesis 3:19).

Jesus does not cause the believer to sweat no longer for his food in the New Covenant. The believer is honorable and works and asks God to give him his daily bread. Jesus lifts humankind and causes us to view our work differently from the way we had done before we became believers. He gives us significance, purpose, and destiny. We are lifted to a place where we no longer work merely to gain wealth, but we work unto the Lord and He blesses whatever we touch (Psalm 1:3). We may sweat and get sore muscles, but we know we are serving Christ and have a new purpose in our labor.

Christians should be the best employees any employer has. They should not always be looking for ways to get over on someone. They shouldn't even be looking for a free meal without working for it. There are always exceptions, and if someone needs help, it is certainly a different matter. But if a believer can work and should work, and doesn't, he is not following the example of Paul or Jesus the Carpenter (Matthew 13:55, Mark 6:3, Acts 20:34, 1 Corinthians 4:12, 11:1).

CLOSING WORD: **"[22] Servants, obey in all things those who are your masters according to the flesh, not just when they are looking, as men pleasers, but in singleness of heart, fearing God. [23] And whatever you** do, work heartily, as for the Lord, and not for men, [24] knowing that from the Lord you will receive the reward of the inheritance; for you serve the Lord Christ." (Colossians 3:22-24)

PRAYER: "Father, help me to be faithful in all of my duties, including my work. Teach me to serve You through my vocation and bring glory to Your name. In Christ's name, I ask this. Amen."

DAY FORTY-FOUR: "Acting like Busybodies."

"[11]For we hear that some among you are leading an undisciplined life, doing no work at all, but acting like busybodies. [12]Now such persons we command and exhort in the Lord Jesus Christ to work in quiet fashion and eat their own bread." (3:11-12)

One drawback of not staying busy doing the right things is that we often fill our time with doing the wrong things. Remember, Paul is giving spiritual and practical advice in this chapter. He is direct here. Paul commands them to cool it. We could paraphrase it somewhat. "Get a job and shut up!" "Eat your own bread and stop mooching off of others."

Being a busybody is meddling in other folks business. This happens in many ways. It is one thing to pray for other folks who are having a tough time. But often even prayer groups get involved in meddling in the affairs of others. We must guard ourselves against this tendency. We generally have enough to deal with in our own families to keep us busy. It's best to resist the desire to know everyone else's business.

We should not tell everything we know about other folks either. Think how much more the Kingdom of God would advance in our time if God's people simply lived by this admonition.

CLOSING WORDS: "**A talebearer reveals secrets, but he who is of a faithful spirit conceals a matter.**" (Proverbs 11:13, NKJV)

PRAYER: "Lord Jesus, help me to mind my own business and do my job. Bless me to be faithful in the right things and resist the wrong. In Jesus' name. Amen."

DAY FORTY-FIVE: "As For You."

"But as for you, brethren, do not grow weary of doing good." (3:13)

Much of life is about sowing and reaping. Paul encouraged these folks to do the right thing and expect a harvest of good to come from it. His advice to them was for them to keep at it. Often we give up when we don't see the results for which we had hoped. We become weary. But we must keep at it. God will bless us as He did these precious believers at Thessalonica if we don't get weary and quit. This is some good Kingdom advice. Hang in there.

CLOSING WORD: "**9 And let us not grow weary while doing good, for in due season we shall reap if we do not lose heart. 10 Therefore, as we have opportunity, let us do good to all, especially to those who are of the household of faith.**" (Galatians 6:9-10)

PRAYER: "Our Father, I need Your help. I often want to see more results from my prayers, my work, and my faith. I get it backward at times. I am guilty of walking by sight and not by faith. Help me to not grow weary in well-doing. Strengthen me to keep doing the right things and trust You with the results. Amen."

DAY FORTY-SIX: "Association."

"If anyone does not obey our instruction in this letter, take special note of that person and do not associate with him, so that he will be put to shame." (3:14)

Taking "special note" of this uncooperative person means to "point them out." This is very unpopular in our time. But that was Paul's instruction for these believers. His goal was to put a stop to their unruly and undisciplined behavior. He instructed the believers to do the right things and stop associating with folks who refuse to do the things Paul taught.

The purpose of the disassociation is to put the unruly brother to shame. What a different philosophy from today. He advises they take action that will get the attention of the rebellious brother. I wonder if our softness today is a reason for our ineffective modern Christianity. Sometimes love must be tough. This is not meanness, as we shall note in the next verse. It is tough, direct, and purposeful.

CLOSING WORD: "**I appeal to you, brothers, to watch out for those who cause divisions and create obstacles contrary to the doctrine that you have been taught; avoid them.**" (Romans 16:17, ESV)

PRAYER: "Father, give me the determination to do the right thing and avoid those who do not. Give me the wisdom to handle the relationships in my life in ways that will advance Your Kingdom and bring glory to You. Amen."

DAY FORTY-SEVEN: "Admonish."

"*Yet* do not regard him as an enemy, but admonish him as a brother." (3:15)

I have met some mean Christians. How about you? Paul is not calling for meanness here. But he is serious about separation. We are identified in our beliefs with those with whom we associate. That is why we must not be a member of a Church that doesn't have a sound biblical doctrine.

We can be direct and tell the truth without being nasty. But we still must not overlook error. The individual in the above text is a believer, not an unbeliever. He is in error. Therefore, in Paul's thinking it was not okay to just believe anything as long as one believes in Jesus too. The correct doctrine was important then and is important now. It helps keep us from the deception Paul talked about in chapter two of this letter.

Therefore, Paul's advice here is connected to the awareness of deception he gave earlier. We do not always know whether the person is a brother in error or a deceived person sent by the devil to cause division. We need discernment. Verse 15 above is advice for how to help an erring brother. "May we too be courageous and faithful to God's counsel."

CLOSING WORD: "**[10]As for a person who stirs up division, after warning him once and then twice, have nothing more to do with him,[11] knowing that such a person is warped and sinful; he is self-condemned.**" (Titus 3:10-11)

PRAYER: "O Father, I am so easily deceived by so many things. Help me to discern the difference between those who are erring brothers and those who are sent by the devil to cause division and deception. Give me the grace to stand firmly and appropriately in either case. O Lord, please restore my erring brother speedily. Almighty God, shut the mouth of those who are sent by the evil one into my life to cause trouble. In Jesus' name. Amen."

DAY FORTY-EIGHT: "Acting in Peace All the Time."

"**Now may the Lord of peace Himself continually grant you peace in every circumstance. The Lord be with you all!**" (3:16)

The Lord of Peace is *Yahweh Shalom* in the Old Testament. The more popular expression is *Jehovah Shalom*. God has always been interested in giving His beloved His peace. We need it every day. We need it for every circumstance. We need to know that the Lord is with us. It says, "The Lord of peace *Himself*." This is very personal. The Prince of Peace promised to give His followers peace (Isaiah 9:6, John 14:27, 16:33). This is a promise every believer should claim for their own, and proclaim over other believers.

These are powerful and comforting words. Paul declared this as a blessing over these believers. He invoked it over them. God instructed the priests in the Old Covenant to invoke peace over the children of Israel (Numbers 6:22-26). So there is a connection between believers invoking peace upon others. Jesus told His disciples to invoke peace upon a house when they entered it. Every believer in the New Covenant is a priest (1 Peter 2:5-10, Revelation 1:6).

All means *all*. God's presence should be apparent in every believer's life. We should not settle for less than seeing all our brothers and sisters walking in the peace of God. Speak peace to the people in your life. Wouldn't it be great if we too were known as those who invoke peace upon God's people and anyone who supports the advancement of His Kingdom?

CLOSING WORD: **"²And He said to them, The harvest indeed is abundant [there is much ripe grain], but the farmhands are few. Pray therefore the Lord of the harvest to send out laborers into His harvest. ³Go your way; behold, I send you out like lambs into the midst of wolves. ⁴Carry no purse, no provisions bag, no [change of] sandals; refrain from [retarding your journey by] saluting *and* wishing anyone well along the way. ⁵Whatever house you enter, first say, Peace be to this household! [Freedom from all the distresses that result from sin be with this family]. ⁶And if anyone [worthy] of peace *and* blessedness is there, the peace *and* blessedness you wish shall come upon him; but if not, it shall come back to you."** (Luke 10:2-6, AMP)

PRAYER: "Father, I thank You for giving me peace through Jesus Christ. Teach me to go forth and proclaim peace to Your people. In Your name I ask. Amen."

DAY FORTY-NINE: "Autographed in Grace."

"I, Paul, write this greeting with my own hand, and this is a distinguishing mark in every letter; this is the way I write. [18] The grace of our Lord Jesus Christ be with you all." (3:17-18)

Paul dictated his letters. He likely did the same here. But it appears he took the pen away from the scribe at this point and personally wrote the benediction and autographed the letter. He wanted it to be a personal letter from him. He told them it had his personal and unusual mark. This might have been done in large letters (Gal. 6:11).

Paul began many of his letters invoking *grace* and *peace* to the people of God, as did others (1 Corinthians 1:3, 1 Peter 1:2, Revelation 1:4). He ends this one invoking peace and grace to these believers. They would need to walk in both, as every believer does. He declared peace to them in verse 16 and grace here in verse 18.

Paul preached the grace of God through Jesus Christ. This is the only gospel. Anything else is a false letter and is deception. The world is full of deception and rebellion. Only the grace of God keeps the people of God (Galatians 1:3-9). "May we all acknowledge this and ask God for more grace every day. Amen."

CLOSING WORD: **"Grace to you and peace from God our Father and the Lord Jesus Christ."** (1 Corinthians 1:3, MEV)

PRAYER: "Father, thank You for saving me by Your grace through faith. Help me to grow in the grace of God every day as I walk with You. In Jesus' Name, I ask. Amen."

DAY FIFTY: "Affirmation and Action."

The power of God's Word is activated as we read, study, and meditate on it, and the Holy Spirit makes it a reality in our lives by the grace of God. Let us affirm what He has revealed to us in this chapter and ask Him to show us how to activate its truth into our daily lives.

WORTHY OF THE KINGDOM

THE WORD FOR TODAY: "⁶ Be anxious for nothing, but in everything by prayer and supplication, with thanksgiving, let your requests be made known to God; ⁷ and the peace of God, which surpasses all understanding, will guard your hearts and minds through Christ Jesus. ⁸Finally, brethren, whatever things are true, whatever things *are* noble, whatever things *are* just, whatever things *are* pure, whatever things *are* lovely, whatever things *are* of good report, if *there is* any virtue and if *there is* anything praiseworthy—meditate on these things. ⁹ The things which you learned and received and heard and saw in me, these do, and the God of peace will be with you." (Philippians 4:6-10)

PRAYER: "Gracious Father, I come to You today not on my own merit, but on the perfect life and holiness of Jesus, my Savior. Show me ways I can increase in understanding and wisdom, and operate in the destiny You have for me. Reveal Your purpose to me each day. Activate me toward Your Kingdom goals. In Christ's name, I ask this. Amen."

THE WORD IN ACTION:

Identify the Kingdom truth God Has affirmed in you during this study of His Word:

_____
_____
_____
_____
_____
_____
_____
_____
_____
_____
_____
_____
_____
_____
_____

Dear Father, please show me how You want to activate this truth in my daily life:

OTHER BOOKS AVAILABLE AT:

Createspace: http://www.createspace.com   (Go to **STORE** drop box and type in name – "Thomas Hendershot")
Amazon: http://www.amazon.com
Amazon Author's Page: Thomas R. Hendershot
Barnes and Noble: http://www.barnesandnoble.com/
Alibris: http://www.alibris.com/booksearch

Doors
Possessing the Land
Ministry to the Sick
Guarding Your Heart and Mind
Psalms, Hymns, and Spiritual Songs
Saints in Strange Situations

Insights for Daily Living Series
Worshiping, Working, and Waiting (First Thessalonians)
Worthy of the Kingdom (Second Thessalonians)

Secrets of the Blessed Life Series
The Blessing in the Valley (Psalm 84)
Covenant Confidence (Psalm 25)
The Shamar Blessing (Psalm 121)
Samach (Psalm 16)

Evangelical Essentials Series
Book One: The Name and Nature of God

Pastoral Perspectives Series
1 Corinthians (1-3): Spiritual Wisdom for the Church
1&2 Thessalonians

Made in the USA
Middletown, DE
22 April 2024

53290142R00044